# Looking Back at the Columbia Gorge

## A Photographic Journey

# Looking Back at the Columbia Gorge

## A Photographic Journey



Special thanks to Mary Ann Burrows of the Wallowa History Center, Wallowa, Oregon, for providing the foundation for the collection of historical photographs that appear in this book. And to Edsel White of Vancouver, Washington, for sharing his personal collection that made the expanded edition possible.

Published by
Bear Creek Press
814 Couch Avenue • Wallowa, Oregon 97885
541-886-9020 • bearcreekpress@eoni.com
www.bearcreekpress.com

Maps ©Bear Creek Press of Wallowa, Oregon

Printing History
Bear Creek Press First Edition: March 2005
Expanded: April 2007
This printing: July 17, 2007

Front Cover
"Approach to Mitchell's Point, Columbia River Highway, Oregon," from the collection of Edsel White, Vancouver, Washington

Back Cover
Motorists along the Columbia River Highway, c. 1915

Printed in the United States of America

ISBN: 1-930111-52-5

Bear Creek Press

World Headquarters located in Wallowa, Oregon U.S.A.
(at the old Abbie Riggle place on Bear Creek Road).

# Contents

"Multitudes have from this point gazed on the wonderful beauty of nature and felt their souls expand and their vision enlarge under the spell of this enchanting spot."

– *Where-To-Go Directory*, 1920
in an entry describing the
Columbia River Gorge

**Columbia River Highway, 1915**

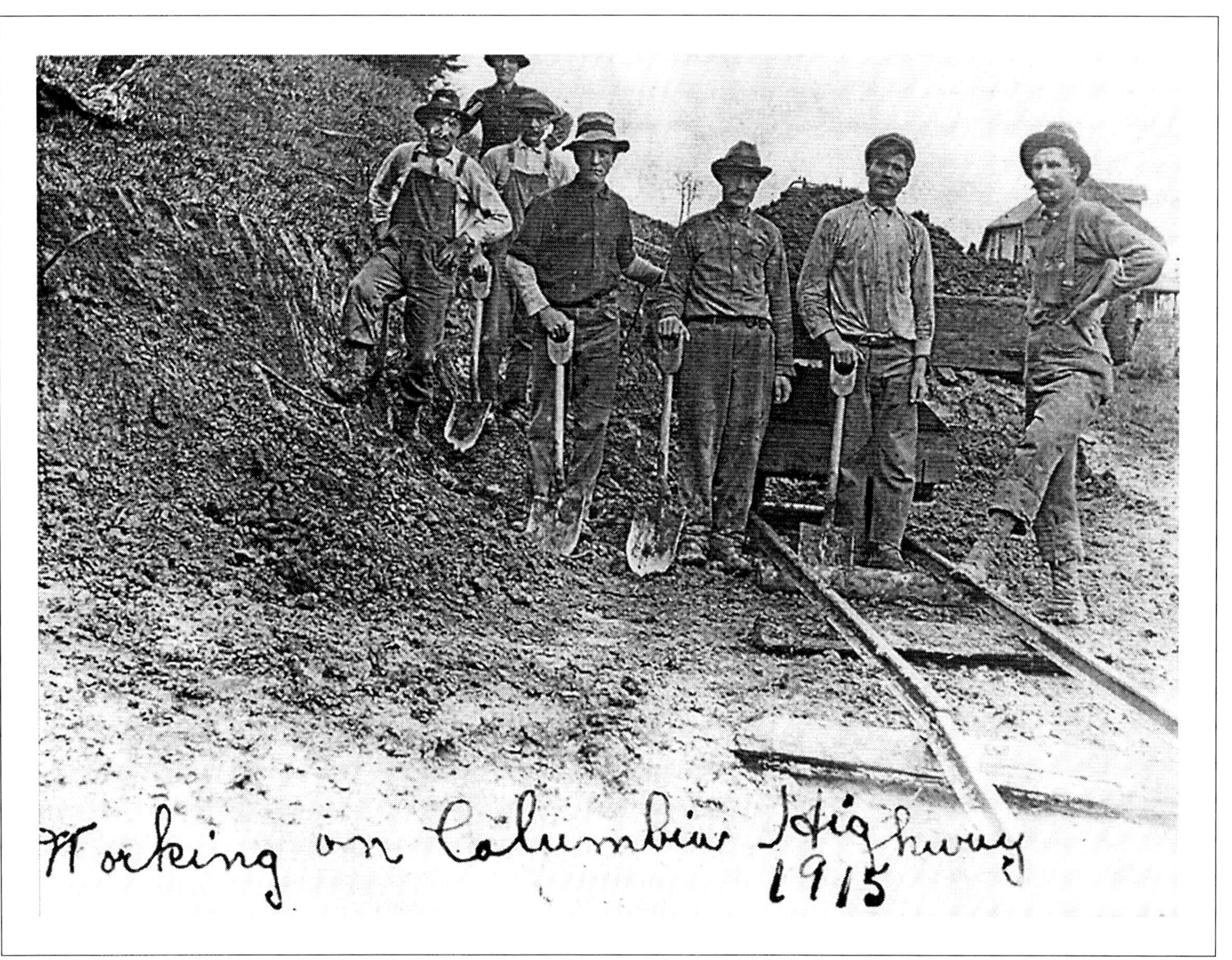
Working on Columbia Highway
1915

# INTRODUCTION

On a long-ago day in a faraway land, an ice-choked river got set to bust loose. What happened next has become the stuff of mythological wonder and geological study, and the reason the Columbia River Gorge has long been a land of enchantment. For on this day less than 20,000 years ago in a glacier-clogged valley that would one day be known as Montana, an ancient lake burst through the ice dam that imprisoned it and began its rush to the sea.

Spanning more than 3,000 square miles and standing as deep as 2,000 feet—more than 500 cubic *miles* of water, an amount greater than the combined flow of all the rivers on Earth multiplied by *ten*—this lake erupted in a raging flood that roared its way westward, shaking the ground and scouring the land along the way. Traveling at a speed of sixty-five miles per hour, the water took only a day to reach the canyon that serves as the one breach in the Cascade Range—the Columbia Gorge.

**Samuel C. Lancaster**

Once squeezed into this basalt funnel, the water rose ever higher, cresting at one point to approximately 1,200 feet—the height of the Empire State Building—and battering away at the canyon walls until streams were left hanging high on the edges of steep cliffs, with nothing left to do but take the long plunge to the bottom. In the flood's wake, the earth crumbled and slumped and slid away, its rock and mud toppling or slipping into the river below and churning the water to a white, stony froth.

Over and over again through the next 2,000 years this drama repeated itself: the glaciers creeping down from the north to plug the river into a lake, the lake at last breaking free to begin its run to the sea, the flood gouging and carving the Gorge into a land of plummeting waterfalls and thundering rapids. It was also a land so wild that for centuries only footpaths and wagon trails crossed it. And then along came Samuel Christopher Lancaster.

"There is a time and place for every man to act his part in life's drama," Lancaster once wrote, "and to build according to his ideals."

For Lancaster, a highway engineer, the time was the second decade of the twentieth century; the place, the Columbia River Gorge; and his ideals, to create in the Gorge what he called a "broad thoroughfare as a frame to the beautiful picture which God created." And so he set out to do what many believed could not be done—build a highway through the Gorge "from Portland east through the Cascade Range."

The surveying started on a September day in 1913, just five years after the first Model T Ford rolled off the assembly line and drove America into the automotive age. "Our first order of business," Lancaster said, "was to find the beauty spots, or those points where the most beautiful things along the line might be seen in the best advantage, and if possible to locate the road in such a way as to reach them." With that noble goal setting the course of the highway's design, construction began in October 1913. Less than two years later, in July 1915, the road was completed from Portland to Hood River, though it would take almost seven more years to finish the highway to The Dalles. (It was officially dedicated on June 7, 1916.)

**Samuel Lancaster (back seat) at Shepperd's Dell in 1915, on the opening of the first segment of the Columbia River Highway**

When the Columbia River Highway was finished—all 73.8 miles, 18 bridges, 7 viaducts, 3 tunnels, and 2 footbridges combined into the first major paved road in the Pacific Northwest—Samuel C. Lancaster had created a masterpiece that many considered a work of art as well as an engineering marvel.

"The best of all great highways in the world, glorified!" exclaimed the *Illustrated London News*. "It is the king of roads!"

The ensuing decades, however, were unkind to Lancaster's creation. When the forerunner of today's Interstate 84 was built along the river bank, more than twenty miles of the Columbia River Highway were destroyed. Much of what was left began to suffer from weather, neglect, and mud slides, as well as from a fear for travelers' safety that resulted in state officials abandoning, filling, or dynamiting some of the old highway's most significant landmarks, including the tunnels at Oneonta Bluff, Mitchell Point, and Mosier. Add to this the changes wrought along the Columbia River by the building of dams and the subsequent drowning of its rapids and falls, and it's clear that the Columbia Gorge now looks much different from what it did in Lancaster's day.

**Part of Samuel Lancaster's road**

Even so, some of the most important things have endured. The waterfalls, the vistas, and fifty miles or so of the original highway still await those who seek quiet paths and serene beauty. As for those parts that are now only memories, we can thank the early-twentieth-century photographers who recorded them on film, who recognized in the land and its road a treasure worth remembering.

To recapture those days, consider this book a journey from west to east along the old highway in a time when the Columbia River still ran free, the means of travel was the Model T, and the invitation of Samuel Lancaster was still open for the taking: "that you will come to the Oregon Country and acquaint your friends with its wonderful beauty."

If you take the journey, along the way you may just catch a glimpse of a world from almost a century ago when you find yourself looking back at the Columbia Gorge.

– Mark Highberger
Editor & Publisher

**Above and right: segments of the Columbia River Highway**

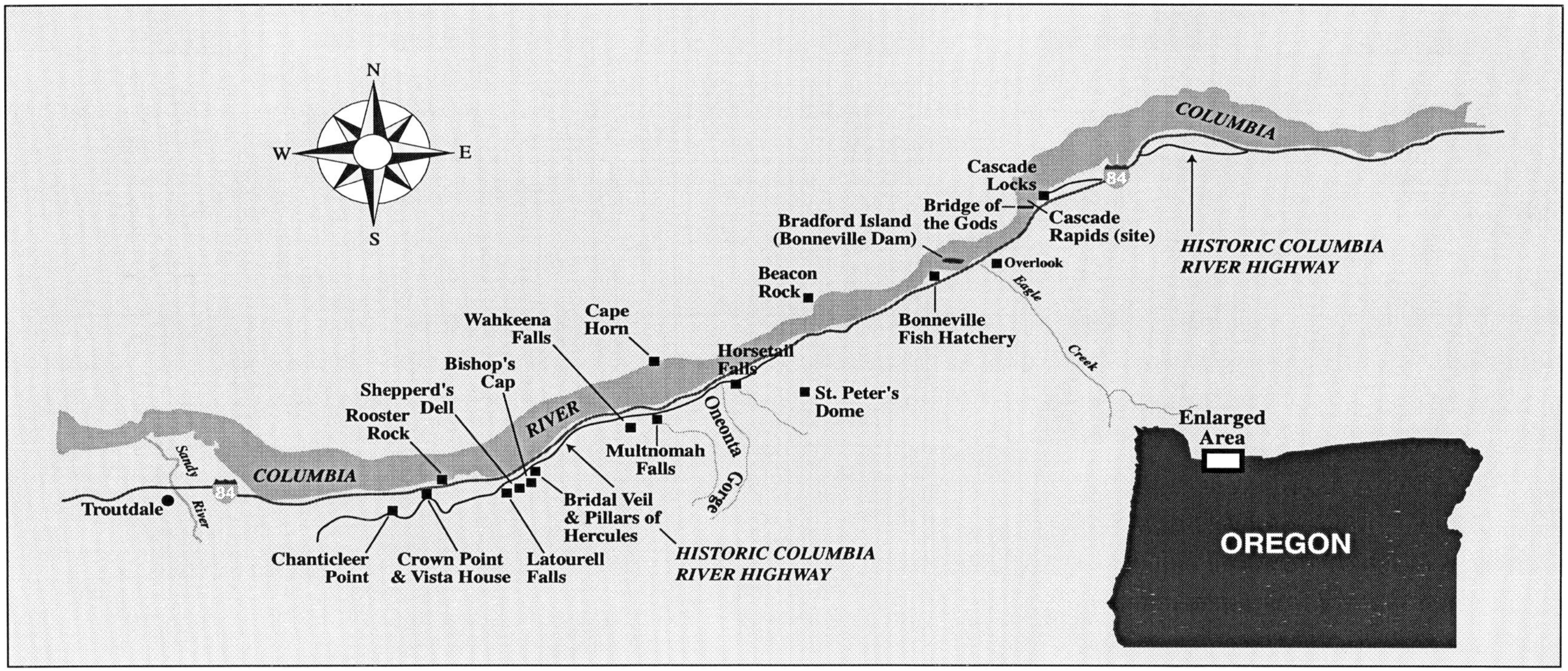

N
W
E
S
COLUMBIA
Cascade Locks
Bridge of the Gods
Cascade Rapids (site)
Bradford Island (Bonneville Dam)
Overlook
Eagle Creek
HISTORIC COLUMBIA RIVER HIGHWAY
Beacon Rock
Bonneville Fish Hatchery
Wahkeena Falls
Cape Horn
Horsetail Falls
St. Peter's Dome
Bishop's Cap
Shepperd's Dell
Rooster Rock
RIVER
Multnomah Falls
Oneonta Gorge
Enlarged Area
Sandy River
COLUMBIA
84
Troutdale
Bridal Veil & Pillars of Hercules
HISTORIC COLUMBIA RIVER HIGHWAY
Chanticleer Point
Crown Point & Vista House
Latourell Falls
OREGON

# Columbia River Gorge — West

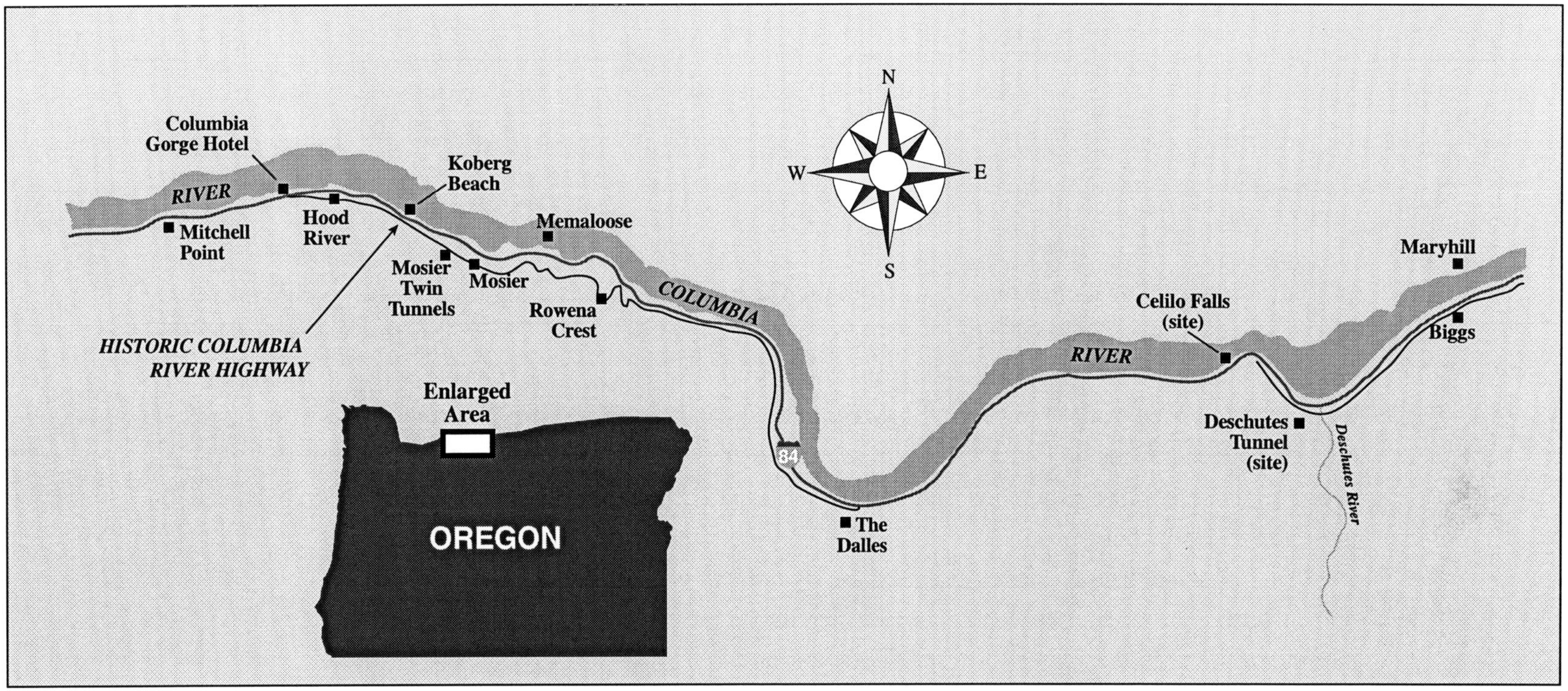

Columbia Gorge Hotel
RIVER
Hood River
Mitchell Point
Koberg Beach
Memaloose
Mosier Twin Tunnels
Mosier
Rowena Crest
COLUMBIA
HISTORIC COLUMBIA RIVER HIGHWAY
Enlarged Area
OREGON
N
W
E
S
84
The Dalles
RIVER
Celilo Falls (site)
Maryhill
Biggs
Deschutes Tunnel (site)
Deschutes River

# Columbia River Gorge — East

Our sail down the Columbia and through the Cascade Mountains altogether was a notable one, and unsurpassed everything in the way of wild and picturesque river scenery that we had seen yet...Piled along the sky on either side, up two or three thousand feet, for fifty miles at a stretch with only a narrow gorge between, the Columbia whirls and boils along through this in supreme mightiness and power; while from the summit of the great walls little streams here and there topple over, run like lace for a time, then break into a million drops and finally come sifting down as mist into the far depths below.

Some of these tiny cascades streaked the cyclopean walls, like threads of silver, from top to bottom. Others seemed mere webs of gossamer, and these the wind at times caught up and swayed to and fro, like veils fit for goddesses. These mountains, all through the cañon of the Columbia, abound with such fairy cascades, whence their name...All along, the vast basaltic walls of the cañon are shaped and fashioned into domes and turrets, ramparts and battlements; and surely in point of picturesque grandeur and effect, the Columbia would be hard to beat.

– Brigadier General James Rusling, 1866

**Chanticleer Inn and Point (today's Women's Forum State Park), Crown Point and Vista House in distance**

**Chanticleer Inn**

**View of Columbia River from Chanticleer Point, including Rooster Rock and cannery below, Crown Point and Vita House to right**

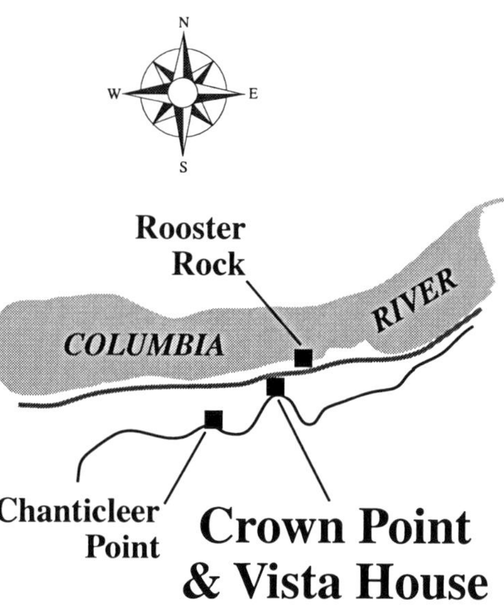
N
W
E
S
Rooster Rock
COLUMBIA
RIVER
Chanticleer Point
Crown Point & Vista House

Crown Point

**Crown Point (before the construction of Vista House)**

**Dedication of Vista House, 1918**

**Dedication of Vista House, 1918**

**Crown Point and Vista House**

**Vista House**

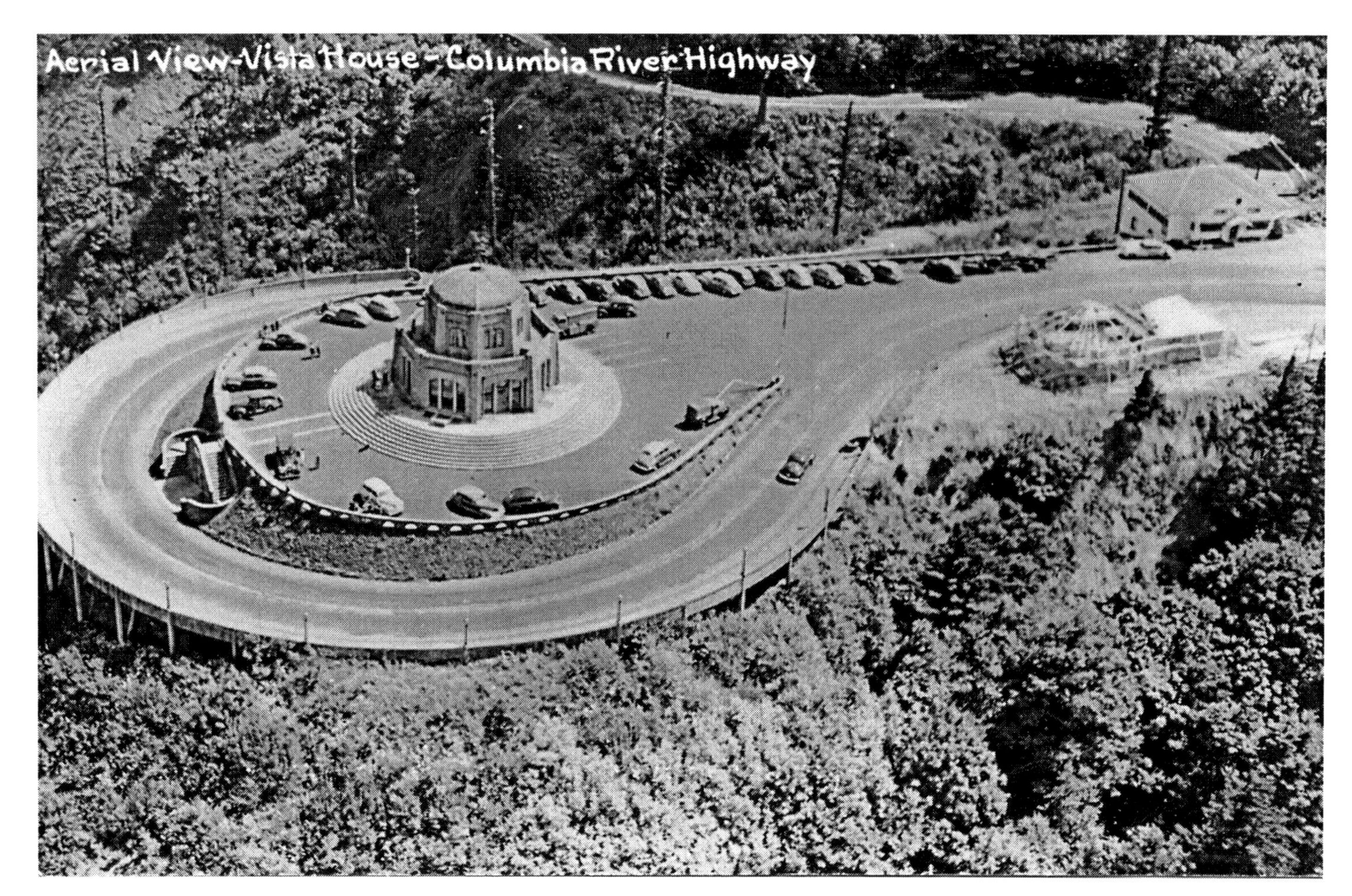


**Vista House**

**Vista House**

**Vista House**

**Rooster Rock and the Columbia River**

**Rooster Rock and sternwheeler**

**Rooster Rock and salmon cannery**

**Bridge near Latourell Falls**

**Road near Latourell Falls**

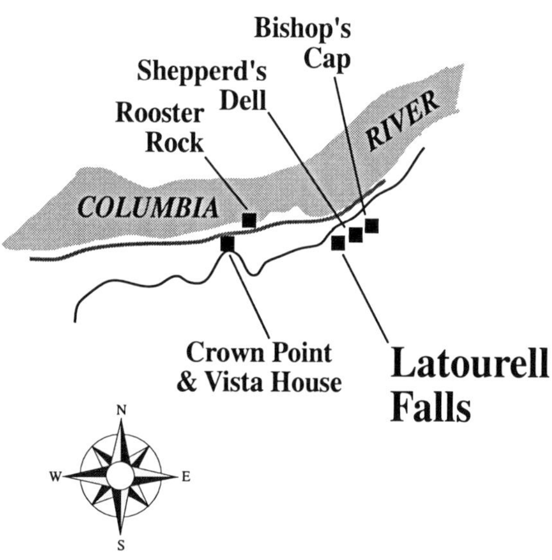


**Latourell Falls**

**Shepperd's Dell**

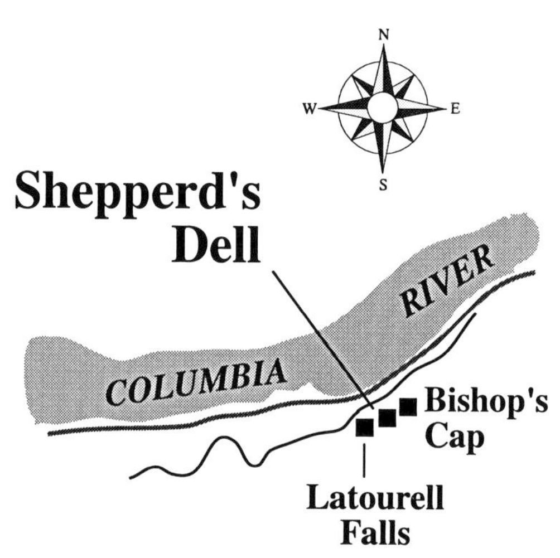


Shepperd's Dell

**Shepperd's Dell**

**Bishop's Cap**

**Bridal Veil Falls**

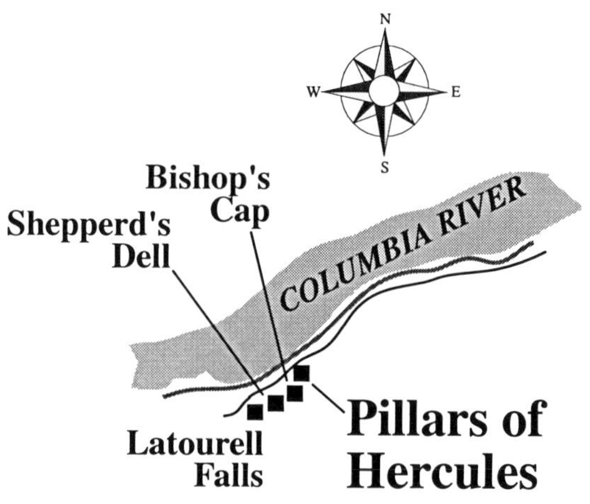


**Pillars of Hercules**

**Pillars of Hercules**

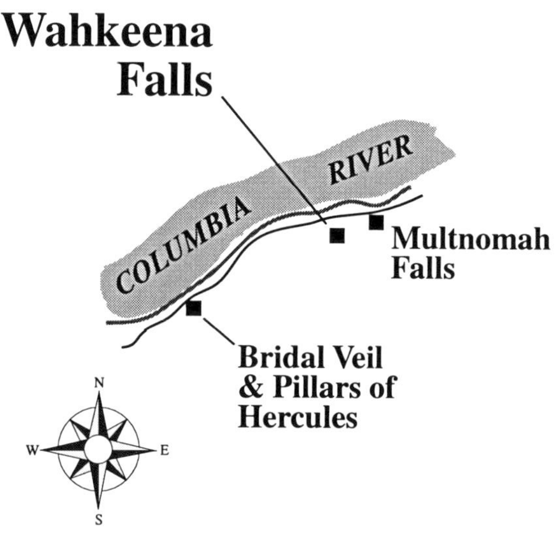


Wahkeena Falls

**Wahkeena Falls**

**Wahkeena Falls trail**

**Columbia River Highway near Multnomah Falls**

**Multnomah Falls**

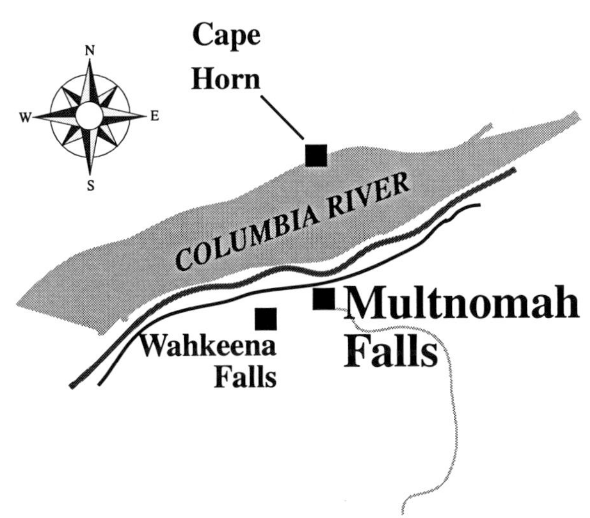


Multnomah Falls & Columbia River Highway

**Multnomah Falls**

**Multnomah Falls Lodge**

**Multnomah Falls**

**Multnomah Falls**

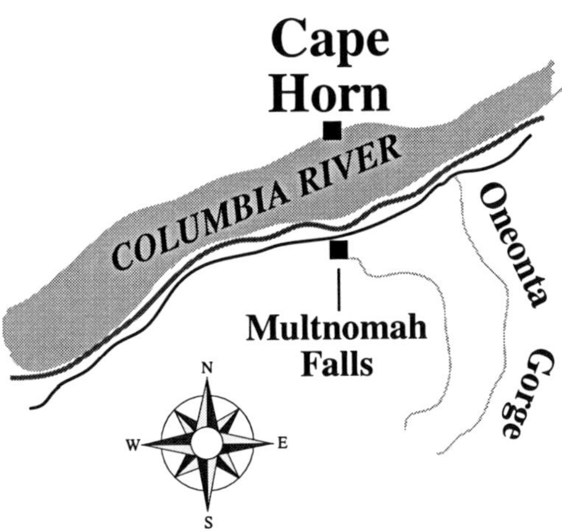
Cape
Horn
COLUMBIA RIVER
Oneonta
Gorge
Multnomah
Falls
N
W
E
S

Cape Horn

**Cape Horn**

**Oneonta Gorge**

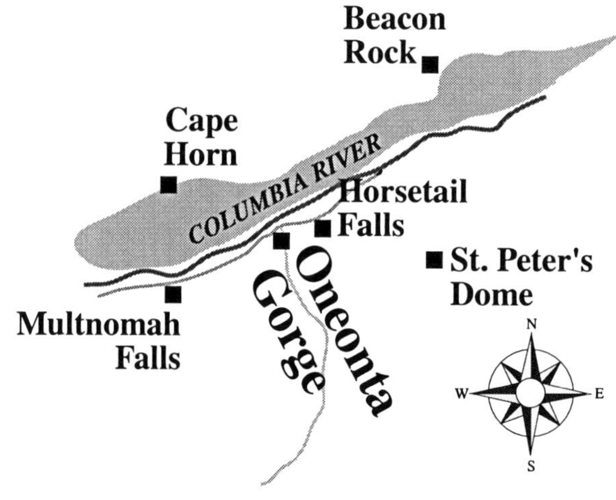


Oneonta Bluff

**Oneonta Tunnel**

**Horsetail Falls**

**St. Peter's Dome**

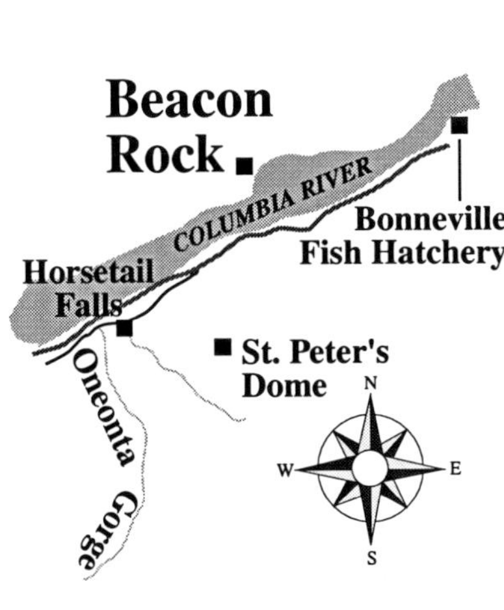
Beacon Rock
COLUMBIA RIVER
Bonneville Fish Hatchery
Horsetail Falls
St. Peter's Dome
Oneonta Gorge
N
W
E
S

Beacon Rock

**Beacon Rock**

**Fish wheel near Beacon Rock**

**Bonneville Fish Hatchery**

**Bonneville Fish Hatchery**

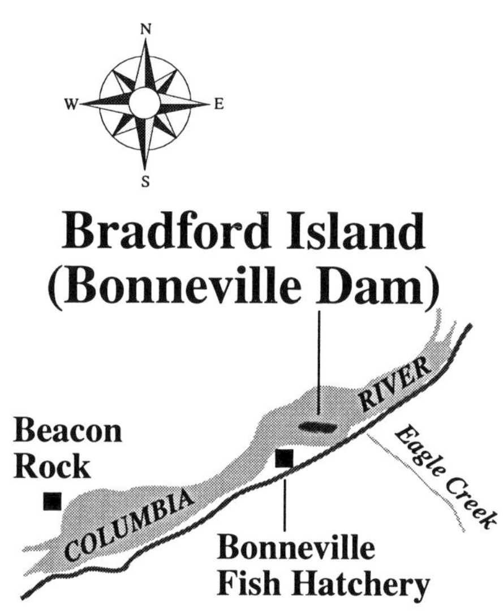


**Bradford Island**
**before construction of Bonneville Dam**
**(inset: 1933 plans for the dam)**

**Bradford Island and Bonneville Dam**

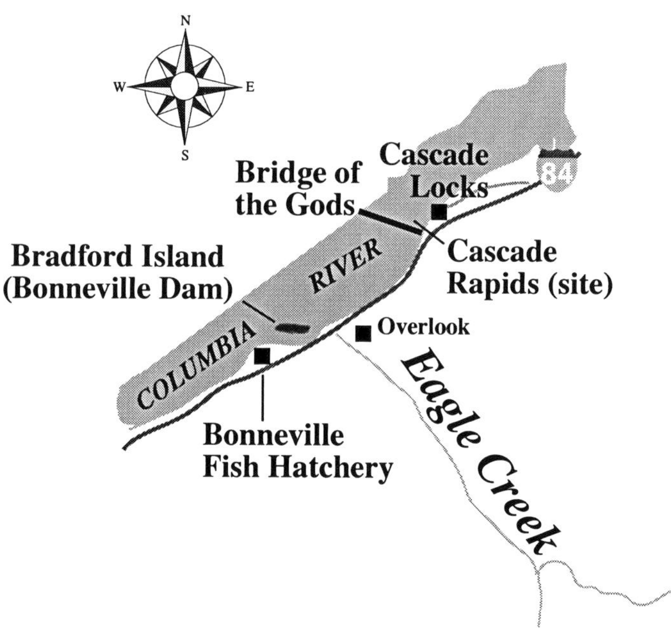


**Columbia River Highway near Eagle Creek**

**Eagle Creek Bridge during its construction**

**Punch Bowl at Eagle Creek**

**Cascade Rapids, 1888**

**Bridge of the Gods under construction, early 1920s**

**Bridge of the Gods, completed in 1926 and raised 44 feet in 1938 to accommodate high waters created by Bonneville Dam**

**Construction of Cascade Locks, 1880s**

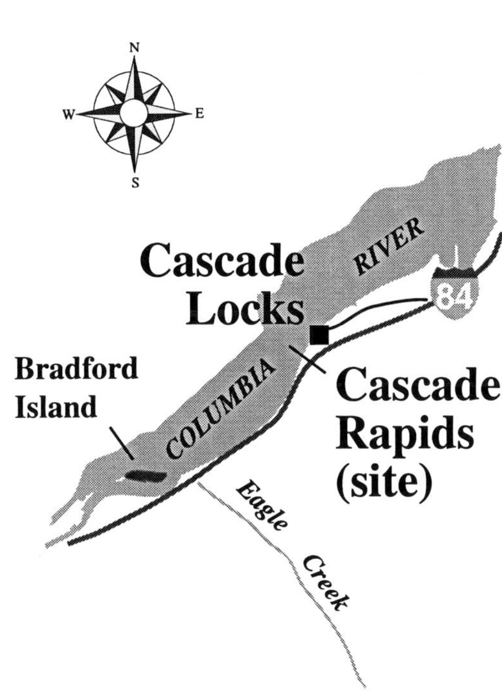


**Construction of Cascade Locks, 1880s**

**Cascade Rapids and Cascade Locks**

**Cascade Rapids and Cascade Locks**

**Cascade Rapids and Cascade Locks**

**The town of Cascade Locks, 1893**

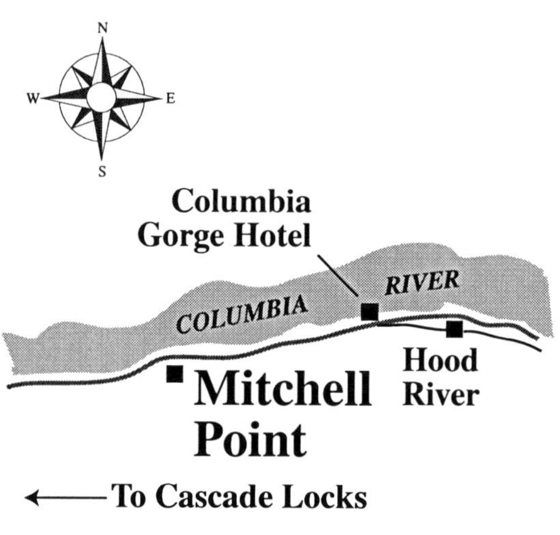


**Viaduct at Mitchell Point Tunnel**

**Mitchell Point Tunnel**

**Mitchell Point Tunnel**

**Mitchell Point Tunnel**

**The opening of the Columbia Gorge Hotel, 1921**

**The Columbia Gorge Hotel, 1921**

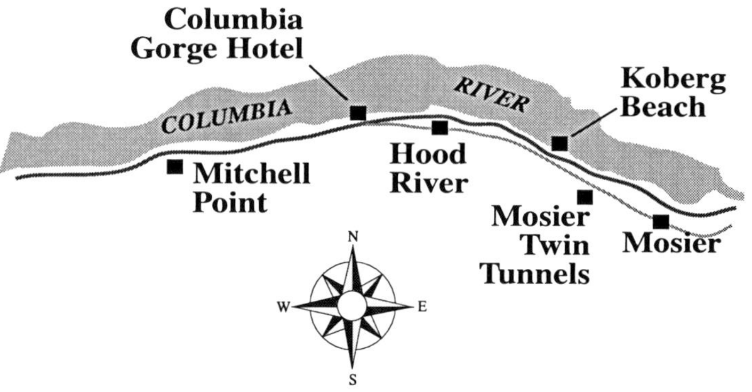


**The Columbia River Highway between Cascade Locks and Hood River**

**Hood River, early twentieth century**

**The Columbia River Highway between Hood River and Mosier**

**Dance pavilion at Koberg Beach**

Mosier, 1912

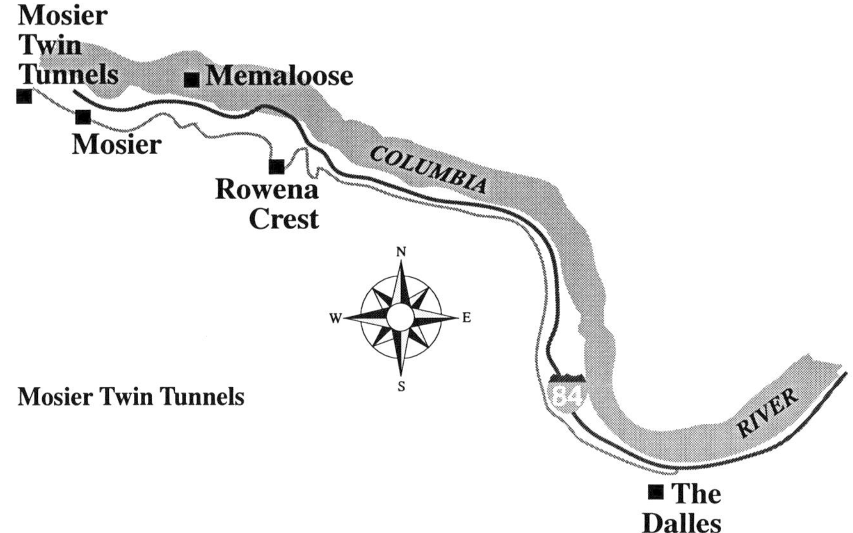


Mosier Twin Tunnels

**Memaloose Island, an ancient Native American burial site**

**Native American remains on Memaloose**

**Rowena Crest & Rowena Loops**

**Rowena Loops**

**Columbia River Highway from Rowena Crest to The Dalles**

**The Dalles, early twentieth century**

**Columbia River at The Dalles**

**Columbia River ferry at The Dalles (ferry closed when bridge opened 1953)**

**Above and right: Celilo Falls**

**Celilo Falls**

**Celilo Falls, 1899**

**Celilo Rapids, 1902**

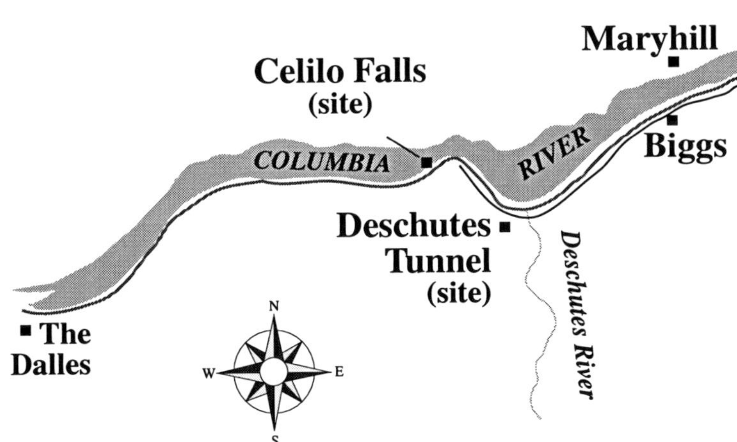

Deschutes Tunnel

**Biggs, early 1950s**

**Biggs-Maryhill ferry, early 1950s (closed when bridge, opposite page, opened 1962)**

**Bridge overBiggs Rapids, upstre am of Celilo Falls and near Biggs**

*Books unique to the Northwest*

Established in 1999, Bear Creek Press of Wallowa, Oregon, specializes in publishing books unique to the Pacific Northwest, especially those that capture the life or preserve the history of the region.

## For more information:



**"There could be nothing so important as a book can be."**
**– Max Perkins**